The Wit & Wisdom of
West Highland Terriers

This edition is created for LOMOND

FLAME TREE
6 Melbray Mews
Fulham, London SW6 3NS
United Kingdom
www.flametreepublishing.com

First edition published 2007

15 17 19 20 18 16
1 3 5 7 9 10 8 6 4 2

The CIP record for this book is available from the British Library.

ISBN: 978 1 84204 487 2

Printed in China

Thanks to: Cat Taylor, Sara Robson and Gemma Walters

The Wit & Wisdom of
West Highland Terriers

Ulysses Brave

LOMOND

Foreword

For years I studied Zen and the
Art of Animal Self-consciousness.
Subsequently I have written a large
number of management, self-help
and philosophical texts over the
years, which have provided useful
advice and inspiration. Here then,
is the latest offering.

Ulysses Brave

Inner calm is a rare, often unrecognized quality.

Confidence is the key to success. When hunting for friends or jobs, always walk with a ready smile and a straight back.

Try to avoid situations
which you find depressing.

Make some time every day to celebrate.

Fear is your greatest
enemy. You can defeat it
by remembering those
who love you.

If you have trouble
concentrating, just take
five deep breaths and
remain still for
two minutes.

Be ready for action at all times, especially in the defence of your places of rest.

*Sometimes the perfect colour
is simply not available.
Try not to put yourself
under too much pressure.*

Don't feel ashamed about
the silly things you do
in the privacy of your
own home.

Twins can be fun!

Curiosity can be a good thing.

Judgement is always better.

If life seems to become entangled, try to do something completely different.

There are times when we all want to sink into the background. Camouflage, correctly administered, can be useful.

Here we go again...

*Opening your lungs first
thing in the morning will
fill your body with
life-enhancing energy.*

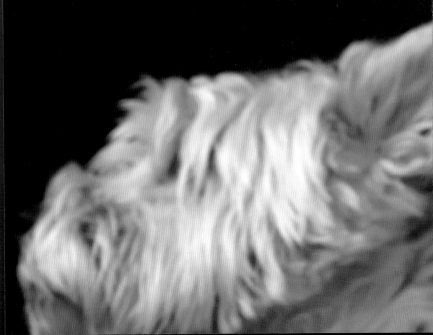

The ancient art of moon-staring
can bring significant benefits
to the inner soul.

Luxuries and privileges
can sometimes hold you back.
It is often better to fight for
what you want.

Just focus on your goals...

...dont wait for events, leap towards them and wrestle them to the ground.

Going to a party can relieve the tension, even if it's the last thing you want to do.

Some people like parties!

*Try to maintain
a healthy diet.*

If you bring a friend to an important event, make sure they don't cramp your style.

Watch and compose yourself
before you leap in. Success
lies in planning and poise.

Dreaming of a better place can help you through the day.

Sometimes it's a great relief
to get to the end of the day.

Keep your spine in a neutral position for as long as you can manage.

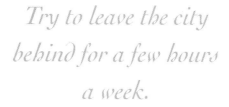

*Try to leave the city
behind for a few hours
a week.*

Some people will be
wary if you show too
much enthusiasm.

Try to find a new challenge in your life.

*If you find yourself in
a tight corner, genuine
curiosity can be the most
disarming weapon.*

*All forms of Martial Arts
provide great discipline.*

You know a true friend
by their attitude to
your appearance.

See you soon ...